Katherine Parr: Henry VIII's Sixth Queen

A Tudor Times Insight

By Tudor Times

Published by Tudor Times Ltd

Tudor Times Insights

Tudor Times Insights collate articles from our website www.tudortimes.co.uk which is a repository for a wide variety of information about the Tudor and Stewart period 1485 – 1625. There you can find material on People, Places, Daily Life, Military & Warfare, Politics & Economics and Religion. The site has a Book Review section, with author interviews and a book club. It also features comprehensive family trees, and a 'What's On' event list with information about forthcoming activities relevant to the Tudors and Stewarts.

www.tudortimes.co.uk

Titles in the Series

Profiles

Katherine Parr: Henry VIII's Sixth Queen

James IV: King of Scots

Lady Margaret Pole: Countess of Salisbury

Thomas Wolsey: Henry VIII's Cardinal

Marie of Guise: Regent of Scotland

Thomas Cromwell: Henry VIII's Chief Minister

Lady Penelope Devereux: Sir Philip Sidney's Muse

James V: Scotland's Renaissance King

Lady Katherine Grey: Tudor Prisoner

Sir William Cecil: Elizabeth I's Chief Minister

Lady Margaret Douglas: Countess of Lennox

Sir James Melville: Scottish Ambassador

Tudors & Stewarts 2015 – A collection of 12 profiles

People

Who's Who in Wolf Hall

Politics & Economy

Field of Cloth of Gold

Succession: The Tudor Problem

The Pilgrimage of Grace and Exeter Conspiracy

Contents

Katherine Parr: Henry VIII's Sixth Wife

Introduction

Katherine Parr is often characterised as the least-well known of Henry VIII's six wives, a nurse to him in old age, and an affectionate step-mother to his children. However, that description is far from a complete portrait of a woman who married four times (once even for love), was an intellectual, a published author and Regent of England. Her influence on her step-daughter Elizabeth I was profound, and she left Elizabeth with a vigorous, and successful example of feminine strength and power in a male-dominated age.

Katherine was the first Queen of England to also be Queen of Ireland, and the first to be buried as a Protestant. She was one of the few members of the Tudor royal family to have lived and travelled outside the south-east of England and was thus a first-hand witness of the Pilgrimage of Grace, and the widening gap between the old, conservative north, and the new, radical south.

Katherine Parr seems to have been a woman of much charm and with a lovable nature. Her step-children were all very fond of her, and she had close relationships with her siblings and cousins. Henry clearly respected her intellect, and she was the first Queen to have her own works published. Her love of shoes and dancing and the pleasure she took in fine clothes and shoes endear her to a modern generation, even while her religious writings that she set so much store by, pass us by.

Part 1 contains Katherine's Life Story and additional articles about her, looking at different aspects of her life, including her relationships with her step-children, the places she lived and the religious writings that were such an important aspect of her life.

Family Tree

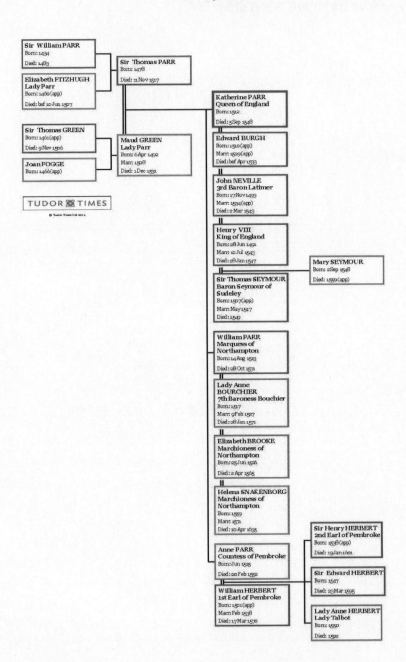

Sir William PARR
Born: 1434
Died: 1483

Elizabeth FITZHUGH
Lady Parr
Born: 1460 (app)
Died: bef 10 Jun 1507

Sir Thomas PARR
Born: 1478
Died: 11 Nov 1517

Sir Thomas GREEN
Born: 1461 (app)
Died: 9 Nov 1506

Joan FOGGE
Born: 1466 (app)

Maud GREEN
Lady Parr
Born: 6 Apr 1492
Marr: 1508
Died: 1 Dec 1531

Katherine PARR
Queen of England
Born: 1512
Died: 5 Sep 1548

Edward BURGH
Born: 1510 (app)
Marr: 1529 (app)
Died: bef Apr 1533

John NEVILLE
3rd Baron Latimer
Born: 17 Nov 1493
Marr: 1534 (app)
Died: 2 Mar 1543

Henry VIII
King of England
Born: 28 Jun 1491
Marr: 12 Jul 1543
Died: 28 Jan 1547

Sir Thomas SEYMOUR
Baron Seymour of
Sudeley
Born: 1507 (app)
Marr: May 1547
Died: 1549

Mary SEYMOUR
Born: 2 Sep 1548
Died: 1550 (app)

William PARR
Marquess of
Northampton
Born: 14 Aug 1513
Died: 28 Oct 1571

Lady Anne
BOURCHIER
7th Baroness Bouchier
Born: 1517
Marr: 9 Feb 1527
Died: 28 Jan 1571

Elizabeth BROOKE
Marchioness of
Northampton
Born: 25 Jun 1526
Died: 2 Apr 1565

Helena SNAKENBORG
Marchioness of
Northampton
Born: 1549
Marr: 1571
Died: 10 Apr 1635

Anne PARR
Countess of Pembroke
Born: Jun 1515
Died: 20 Feb 1552

William HERBERT
1st Earl of Pembroke
Born: 1501 (app)
Marr: Feb 1538
Died: 17 Mar 1570

Sir Henry HERBERT
2nd Earl of Pembroke
Born: 1538 (app)
Died: 19 Jan 1601

Sir Edward HERBERT
Born: 1547
Died: 23 Mar 1595

Lady Anne HERBERT
Lady Talbot
Born: 1550
Died: 1592

TUDOR ✦ TIMES
© Tudor Times Ltd 2016

Katherine Parr's Life Story

Chapter 1: Birth and Childhood (1512 to 1529)

Katherine was born sometime in the summer of 1512 to Sir Thomas Parr and his wife Maud. At that time no-one could have foretold the child's regal destiny, for the Parrs were of that rank of Tudor courtiers known as the 'new men' - well connected, but not rich or powerful, and totally dependent on the will of the sovereign for advancement and wealth. Both Sir Thomas and Lady Parr were loyal servants of the king and queen, he as an ambassador and trusted emissary of Henry VIII, and she as one of Queen Katharine of Aragon's most favoured ladies in waiting. The baby was named Katherine, and, since it was customary to seek a godparent of the highest possible rank amongst the family's circle of acquaintance and to name the child after her, it seems likely that the Queen herself stood as young Katherine Parr's godmother.

Tradition has it that Katherine was born in the Parr family seat of Kendal Castle, but modern scholarship suggests this is unlikely - the castle had been a semi-ruin for 30 years and Sir Thomas and his wife were settled in the south in a variety of houses around the capital and court.

The most likely place for Katherine's birth was near Blackfriars in London where her father had a house and where Sir Thomas and Lady Parr were later buried at St Ann's Church.

Ladies in waiting worked on a roster, and were not always on duty, but once such a prestigious and influential position had been gained, a woman would be most unlikely to give up the chance of advancing her family by retiring. Maud would have returned to her duties as soon as possible, leaving Katherine in the care of nurses. The Parrs went on to have two further children who survived childhood, William, later Marquess of Northampton, and Anne, later Countess of Pembroke. The three Parr children were brought up together and remained close all their lives.

The chance to expand the family further was denied when Sir Thomas, who was some fourteen years older than his wife, died in 1517, leaving Maud a widow at the age of twenty-eight. Unusually, Lady Parr did not remarry but managed both her own estates (she had inherited a very handsome holding from her grandfather, Thomas Green of Green's Norton), and those of her children. Maud was supported in the upbringing of her children by her brother-in-law, Sir William Parr of Horton, and a distant Parr cousin, the influential Bishop of Durham, Cuthbert Tunstall. Katherine, only five on her father's death, clearly looked to both of these men for fatherly guidance throughout her life.

The young Parrs lived for a time with their uncle's family at Rye House in Hertfordshire, together with Sir William's daughter, Maud, later Lady Lane and another cousin Elizabeth Cheyney, later Lady Vaux. They were joined, as was customary at the time, by other young men and Lady Parr arranged the education of all of her young charges. Her establishment received high praise for educating young men in French and other languages.

There has been some dissension over the level of education Katherine received in her childhood. It was becoming fashionable amongst the upper classes to educate girls to a much higher degree than in earlier times, as Humanism began to sweep through the elite of Europe. Katherine certainly learned the standard curriculum of a well-born girl: reading, writing, French (her parents were both reputed to be particularly skilled speakers), needlework and housewifely skills. She may have learnt Latin at this period, she definitely studied it in more detail, together with Spanish and Italian, in later life. There is a charming anecdote, with no factual support whatsoever, that she objected to learning to sew after being told by a fortune teller that she was destined for greater things. She told her mother that, as her hands had been made for sceptres, she had no need for needle and thread. No doubt, if the story is true, Lady Parr soon put her straight – after all, Queen Katharine of Aragon was not too exalted to sew her husband's shirts.

Chapter 2: Mistress Burgh (1512 – 1533)

The primary secular duty of everyone in the late Middle Ages and early Tudor period was to advance the family unit, which generally meant the family as represented by the oldest son. The part of a daughter was to marry well, to increase the influence of her family. Although compatibility of age and tastes might be considered, as love following marriage was considered desirable, her parents made the choice and obedience was expected to be absolute.

Lady Parr took her duty of arranging a match for her eldest daughter seriously. She began negotiations with the Scrope family, via Lord Dacre, grandfather of the intended groom, Henry. Unfortunately, despite Lord Dacre's enthusiasm for the match, his son-in-law, Lord Scrope, seems to have been unimpressed with the notion of Katherine as a match for his son and made unreasonable demands. In particular, he demanded that he would be able to retain Katherine's dowry, should the marriage not take place because of an early death on the part of his son. Clearly Maud could not accept this, as Katherine would then have been unmarried and unprovided for, so negotiations were broken off. Perhaps Lord Scrope had had a premonition, or knew that his son was in poor health, as he did indeed die young, although the draft marriage contract had provided for Katherine to marry any surviving younger brother in such a case.

Lady Parr's next matrimonial scheme was more successful, and Katherine was married in 1529 to Edward Burgh, son of Sir Thomas Burgh of Gainsborough Hall, in Lincolnshire.

Traditional stories that she was married to an old man have their roots in a confusion between young Edward and his grandfather, Sir Edward Burgh. Katherine travelled to north Lincolnshire to live with her new in-laws, in a family that appears to have had what we might nowadays called dysfunctional elements. Old Sir Edward had been mentally disturbed, as had his younger son. The wife of young Edward's brother fell out with Sir Thomas and was thrown out of the house with her children on a charge of adultery. Sir Thomas himself appears to have dominated his family entirely. Katherine was probably glad to form her own household at Kirton-in-Lindsey after a couple of years.

The picture of Katherine as stuck in the country, far from London life and penned up with recluses and lunatics, although an appealing story, is not true. Sir Thomas was at the forefront of radical thought and a strong supporter of Henry VIII's divorce. His religious views were distinctly reformist and he became Chamberlain to Anne Boleyn and a stout resister of the Pilgrimage of Grace.

Katherine's biographers differ on whether this was the time in her life when she became influenced by religious reformers. Her father had died before religious reformation was more than a talking point at the dinner parties of intellectuals such as Sir Thomas More, and her mother remained a faithful servant of Queen Katharine up until her own death on 1531, so it is unlikely that Katherine would have picked up any evangelical ideas from her. It is difficult to believe that Katharine, only seventeen and in the home of a domineering man would not have been influenced by him, especially if he favoured her over his other daughter-in-law. Whatever Sir Thomas Burgh's influence over Katherine was, it proved short-lived, as Edward Burgh died in the spring of 1533 in his early twenties, leaving Katherine widowed before she was twenty-one.

There is more on Katherine's religious views in Chapter 10.

Chapter 3: First Widowhood (1533 to 1534)

In accordance with her marriage articles, once widowed, Katherine had a small dower to live on, drawn from three manors in the south of England. However, the idea of living alone as a 20 year old woman with no children was unthinkable. With her mother dead, her brother in the household of Henry VIII's illegitimate son, Henry Fitzroy, Duke of Richmond, and her sister in the service of Queen Anne Boleyn, there was no family home for Katherine to retreat to. Tradition has it that she went to live with her cousin, Sir Walter Strickland's, widow at Sizergh Castle in Kendal.

This lady was Katherine Neville. Her first marriage to Sir Walter Strickland had produced a son, Sir Thomas, but on widowhood, Katherine Neville married Henry Burgh, the brother of Sir Thomas Burgh of Gainsborough, and thus became the aunt-by-marriage of Katherine Parr's husband. On being widowed a second time, a year or so after Katherine Parr married into the Burgh family, Katherine Neville returned to Sizergh to live with her son. This dual connection with Katherine Parr, make a sojourn at Sizergh very plausible. Such a living arrangement for Katherine Parr would not have been seen as more than a short period of reflection following the loss of her husband. Remarriage was inevitable.

As a widow, with no living parents and a younger brother who had only just reached his majority, Katherine would have had considerable control over the choice of a second husband, though she probably took counsel from Sir William Parr and Bishop Tunstall. However it was made, the choice fell on John Neville, 3rd Baron Latimer.

Chapter 4: Lady Latimer (1534 to 1542)

If he was Katherine's own choice, Lord Latimer was perhaps a rather surprising selection. He was another of the vast Neville family (which seems to have been the most prolific family in all of English history!) and Katherine's second cousin, once removed. At the time of his marriage to Katherine, he was about 40, and had spent most of his life in the north, taking part in Henry VIII's various military jaunts against the Scots, and only visiting London to attend Parliament from time to time, which he seems to have disliked, preferring to stay on his own estates. If this reluctance to travel was known to Katherine, she must have resigned herself to the improbability of seeing much of her own family, all based in the south.

Latimer had been married twice previously and was the father of a son, John, at thirteen, some eight years younger than his new step-mother, and Margaret, aged about eleven. It is apparent that young John had all of the attributes of a sulky teenager, before the term had even been invented. Katherine's later writings about young people as *"...offended at small trifles, taking everything in evil part, grudging and murmuring against their neighbour"* sound heartfelt. Margaret, on the other hand, became devoted to her step mother, was strongly influenced by her, and stayed with Katherine until her own early death aged twenty.

Katherine settled down with her new family, mainly at Lord Latimer's seat of Snape Castle in Yorkshire. There were no children, but the couple seem to have been fond of each other, and Latimer trusted her enough to leave her well provided for in his will, and as the guardian of his daughter.

Latimer is generally described by Katherine's biographers as a man of conservative religious outlook, unlikely to have encouraged any interest in reformist thought and sympathetic to the cause of the Pilgrimage of Grace. However, Dr David Starkey points out that Latimer's daughter, Margaret, was betrothed to the son of Sir Francis Bigod, a radical reformer who was strongly influenced by Bishop Hugh Latimer, (later burned for heresy). Perhaps Lord Latimer was more torn between the old and the new than has been supposed. He had been a member of the Council in the North since 1530, and thus part of the regional government.

Katherine no doubt believed that she would live the quiet life of a country lady, perhaps occasionally visiting the court when her husband travelled south to attend Parliament, perhaps she also hoped for children of her own. But her tranquil country life was soon to be rudely shattered: not long after her marriage, the whole of the north of England was engulfed in the most wide ranging and serious rebellion of the whole Tudor period. Only the canny (not to say deceitful and treacherous) skill of Henry VIII, his chief minister, Thomas Cromwell, and the leader of the army sent against the rebels, Thomas Howard, 3rd Duke of Norfolk, prevented full scale civil war.

The Yorkshire contingent of the Pilgrimage laid siege to Snape Castle and forced Latimer to join its ranks. He took the Pilgrims' oath, later protesting to Henry that it had been under duress and that his purpose was to try to bring the rebels to a more obedient frame of mind. Nevertheless, it is certainly likely that his personal sympathies lay with the Pilgrims and his protestations of coercion do not ring entirely true. Following the disbanding of the Pilgrims, in early December 1536, Latimer returned home, but then left Katherine and his children again in the following January to plead for forgiveness in person at Court.

Unfortunately, however, this act was seen by unreconciled rebels as a betrayal, and a group of them again laid siege to Snape Castle with Katherine and her step-children inside, to try to coerce Latimer to remain true to their cause. There is no record of Katherine or young Margaret suffering any personal attack or violation during this siege, although they must have been terrified, and of course, the fate of many women in war is only too well-known. Hopefully, in the spirit of the Pilgrimage of Grace, they were not ill-treated, and nothing in Katherine's writings suggests any specific violence to her person although Snape Castle was ransacked. Latimer was at his wits' end – not knowing whether to return to Snape, or continue his journey to Doncaster in fulfilment of the King's orders. He elected to return to Snape, where he persuaded the rebels to leave, before racing, post-haste, to Pontefract to rendezvous with Norfolk.

Katherine's views on the Pilgrimage were, presumably, mixed. If she were already leaning toward religious reform, the aims of the Pilgrims would probably have seemed wrong (although Latimer's reformist friend, Sir Francis Bigod was one of the ring-leaders of the second wave of revolt). Additionally, her parents had been loyal servants of the Crown and her brother William was in the King's army, sent to overcome the rebellion. On the other hand, she had spent eight years in the more conservative counties of Lincolnshire, Westmoreland and Yorkshire, in the shadow of the great abbey of Jervaulx which was less than ten miles from Snape and with little opportunity to extend any evangelical leanings. She may also have been influenced by her husband's traditional outlook.

When the rebellion was finally vanquished, with great brutality, Latimer was lucky to escape with his life. He sent ingratiating letters to Cromwell with various presents and fortunately, a good word was put in for him by Norfolk who wrote to Cromwell that there was no evidence against Latimer and that he had acted under duress.

A plea of duress had not saved others, but Latimer was spared. He settled his family in the south, firstly at Wick in Worcestershire, then at a new manor he purchased in Stowe, Northamptonshire. This house was within a few miles of the homes of Katherine's uncle, Sir William Parr of Horton, his daughter, Lady Lane's home at Oldingbury, and the Harrowden estate, presided over by Katherine's cousin Elizabeth Cheyney, now married to Thomas, Lord Vaux. However, Latimer did not spend a lot of time with Katherine in their new home. He was called upon to continue service for the King on the Scottish border and on the numerous commissions that were set up to try and to hang the rebels from the Pilgrimage of Grace.

Following Cromwell's fall in 1542, Latimer recovered his London home near the Charterhouse (which Cromwell had taken a fancy to), and was there during the winter of 1541 - 2 to attend Parliament, accompanied by Katherine. Whether Latimer was worn out by stress, or caught an illness during his frequent journeys is unknown, but he lapsed into ill health at this point, and left Katherine a widow for the second time in March 1543.

Chapter 5: Second Widowhood

Latimer died on 2nd March 1543 at the Latimers' Charterhouse home. It is not clear whether Katherine was with him throughout his illness, or whether she had begun to spend time at Court with the Lady Mary (as Henry's elder daughter was now known, having been demoted from the rank of Princess).

Katherine's biographers differ as to whether Katherine was actually a paid, permanent member of the Princess's Privy Chamber, an 'extraordinary' member who attended the Princess from time to time, but did not need to be paid, or just a guest. There are certainly no records of payment of any salary to her, and Porter contends that this means she could not have been an official Lady in Waiting. James, on the other hand, cites a note in Henry's accounts, for clothes and material for Mary, with Katherine's request that the Henry's accounts department pay the bill as evidence that she was employed by the Princess.

Whatever her official role, Katherine was in a position to catch the eye of new suitors and she soon had two men courting her.

Katherine was very much taken, as was proven in later life, with the charms of the dashing Sir Thomas Seymour, brother of the late Queen Jane Seymour. Seymour was described as handsome with a magnificent voice, but *somewhat empty of matter*. The contrast with the old-fashioned Latimer, twenty years her senior and a nervous wreck following the Pilgrimage of Grace, could hardly have been greater.

However, Katherine was unable to accept Seymour's proposals, as the eye of the King had fallen upon her. Before long, he was sending gifts and visiting her daily. By summer 1543 her fate was sealed and she married Henry as his sixth wife.

It is impossible to accurately gauge Katherine's emotions – she must have been terrified, remembering the recent fates of Anne Boleyn and Katheryn Howard, yet the opportunity to be Queen, to raise her family to undreamed of heights, and perhaps, to lead Henry towards further reform of the Church cannot have failed to allure.

In any event, she had little choice. Even if her family did not press her into such an advantageous match, Henry would not take no for an answer. On 12th July, 1543, Katherine was married in the Queen's Closet at Hampton Court, and became Queen of England. At her marriage, she was attended by her sister, Anne, Lady Herbert, her step-daughter, Margaret Neville, and her two new step-daughters, the Ladies Mary and Elizabeth, as well as Lady Margaret Douglas, Henry's niece and a great favourite at court.

Chapter 6: Queen of England (1543 to 1547)

Katherine set about the business of being Queen with great aplomb. During the first year or two, it was clear that Henry doted on her, lavishing her with gifts of clothes and jewels, (many of which had belonged to Katheryn Howard) as well as settling an impressive jointure on her. She ordered clothes and shoes (some 43 pairs in a variety of sumptuous materials), perfumes, beautiful furnishings and jewels. She had her greyhounds fed on milk and her parrot on hempseed. Porter interprets this creation of a materially beautiful setting as Katherine striving to keep Henry's physical interest in her strong, particularly the orders for herbs and flowers. James' view inclines more to the idea that the herbs and flowers were to hide the stench from Henry's diseased leg, and that the dresses and jewels were rather in the way of a consolation prize. On a more domestic note, Katherine had a spaniel, named Rig, which sported a crimson velvet collar, studded with gold.

For the first eighteen months of her marriage, Katherine rode high. She was praised on all sides, and described by a Spanish visitor to court in 1544:

'The Queen has a lively and pleasing appearance and is praised as a virtuous woman.'

Foreign ambassadors also noted her gracious behaviour towards the Lady Mary, who now lived at Court with her, and her pious and well-regulated household. They reported that the Queen loved to dance and enjoyed music and that the King continued to dote on her.

The culmination of this period of marital bliss came in 1544 when Henry appointed Katherine as Regent whilst he embarked on another of his fantastical forays into France, hoping to emulate Henry V. Katherine was to rule, aided by a Regency Council – this mark of respect shows clearly that Henry cherished and respected Katherine and relied on her loyalty and sense, as he had on that of his first Queen, thirty years before, when sallying into France.

Katherine lived up to his expectations and showed herself a competent and sensible manager – overriding the Council where she felt it was required, but carefully deferring decisions that were too contentious to Henry.

Perhaps this brief period of power went to her head a little, as, after Henry's return, she began to become more involved in questions of religion in a time when to contradict the King's views (which seem to have veered back and forth between Catholicism without the Pope, and a mildly Lutheran interpretation of Humanism) could quickly send a man to the gibbet as a Catholic traitor, or the fire as a heretic.

Henry had always enjoyed religious disputation, even before the divorce proceedings of the 1520s and he and Katherine obviously discussed religion frequently. Perhaps it was these conversations that led her to ponder matters more deeply, or perhaps the seeds of reform had been sown in her mind long before, in Lincolnshire. Whatever the basis for her interest, Katherine became more and more drawn to reform, seeming to move beyond the Lutheran position of most of the reformers at Henry's court, towards Calvinism. She wrote various prayers, including one for *'men to say on entering into battle'* that was probably created for Henry's French campaign in 1544. She also probably undertook the translation of Bishop Fisher of Rochester's *Psalms and Prayers taken out of Holy Scripture*, which translation was published in 1544 by the King's Printer. The first publication of her own creation was *Prayers or Meditations* in 1545.

Not content with translation and writing, Katherine began to involve herself more directly in religious matters, intervening in a case brought to the Court of Alderman in London, in which the widower of one of her servants was charged with voicing heretical opinions and printing radical books. Unfortunately, however, Katherine had enemies – perhaps not so much of her personally, as of her increasingly well-known move towards radical religion. The conservative faction at court, led by Stephen Gardiner, Bishop of Winchester, was determined to keep Henry from the clutches of the Protestants, and, as the king grew older, more paranoid and more irascible, the conservatives plotted to remove his dangerously reformist Queen.

The conservatives had a turn in their luck when Katherine played into their hands by arguing too vigorously with Henry in early 1546. He had obviously become tired of her growing inclination to preach to him, and, when she left the room he allegedly complained to Gardiner that '*It was a good hearing when women become such clerks and a thing much to my comfort to come in mine old days to be taught by my wife.*' Gardiner leapt at the opening and received Henry's permission to investigate Katherine for heresy. Investigations were made into some of the young men at Court who were accused of '*disputing indiscreetly of scripture*' during discussions in the Queen's household. The crux of the investigation, however, soon centred around Katherine's supposed relationship with a young Lincolnshire woman, named Anne Askew.

Anne Askew, a young woman of around twenty-five years old, and a native of Lincolnshire, was one of the most radical, and bravest, religious martyrs of the age. By 1546, she was becoming notorious for her evangelical faith, and her inability to keep quiet about it. She was interrogated in front of the Lord Mayor about her beliefs, and arraigned for heresy. Owing to lack of witnesses she was released, but, failing to be warned, Askew, would not, or could not keep her views to herself. She was again arraigned for heresy in June 1546, and now, the conservative councillors saw their chance.

The ladies of Queen Katherine's household, including Anne, Countess of Hertford, Katherine Willoughby, Duchess of Suffolk and Joan Champernowne, Lady Denny were suspected of supporting Askew, not just with money for her maintenance in gaol, which Anne admitted, but in her opinions. Gardiner and his cohorts were determined to find a link between Askew and the Queen which would send Katherine to the flames.

Shocking even to the hardened courtiers of Henry VIII, Anne was tortured on the rack, with the Lord Chancellor, Wriothesley and Sir Richard Rich personally turning the wheel to try to force her to confess to support from the Queen. Askew defied them all. She refused to incriminate anyone else and was burnt, maintaining her religion to the end.

Undaunted, Gardiner told Henry that the king was *cherish(ing) a viper in his bosom*,' and that he would provide proof of Katherine's heresy. Henry agreed that the Queen could be arrested and investigated.

Somehow, Katherine got wind of what was in store, probably through her doctor. It seems likely that Henry himself had told the doctor, presumably with the intent that Katherine should hear about it. It was not the first time Henry had allowed action to be taken against one his favourites, only for the accusers to find themselves foiled at the last minute. Katherine reacted with predictable terror. She fell into a serious state of panic and grief. Henry, hearing of this, visited her and, having heard that she was worried that she had displeased him, comforted her. All was not complete, however. The next day, speedily recovered, Katherine visited Henry. He began to draw her into controversial topics, but Katherine had rapidly learnt her lesson. She declined to dispute, saying that she was only a *'silly woman'* who desired to learn from her husband. On him taxing her with the suggestion that *'she was become a Doctor to instruct us and not...to be instructed or directed by us'* she immediately was all contrition and claimed that he had misunderstood. She only argued to take his thoughts off his recent illness, and so that she might learn from him.

Henry was clearly fond of Katherine, and perhaps was mindful of the idea that disposing of yet another wife would make him a laughing-stock. Perhaps too, he wanted the domestic peace and harmony that she had given to his family to continue. Whether he was really convinced that she had no heretical leanings must be a moot point. He was no fool, and had heard enough flattery in his life to recognise it. Nevertheless, he affected to believe her, declaring that they were *'perfect friends again.'*

From this time on, Katherine's political influence seems to have diminished. Henry continued to cosset her, but she was careful to play the part of the obedient wife. The change in their relationship can perhaps be seen in the contents of Henry's final Will. In his Will of 1544, Katherine was named as Regent for the Prince Edward, should Henry not return from France, but by late 1546 he had drawn up a new Will, with no mention of Katherine as Regent, but provision for a Regency Council.

During the last months of 1546 Katherine spent some time with Henry, but at Christmas of that year they parted, she to spend Christmas at Greenwich with her step-daughter Mary, and he at Hampton Court with only a few of his closest Councillors. She had never been parted from him at Christmas before, and perhaps knew that this heralded the end.

On 28th January 1547, Henry died. It is unlikely that Katherine was present during his final days.

Chapter 7: Queen Dowager (1547 to 1548)

Henry, even though he had dropped Katherine from any involvement in a Regency government, treated her well in his Will. He left her several houses, a substantial amount of money and her jewels, and ordered that she be treated as Queen for the rest of her life. Katherine retired to her home at Chelsea, accompanied by her younger step-daughter Elizabeth, and, to outward appearance, began an appropriate period of mourning. In secret, however, she was already receiving the attentions of Sir Thomas Seymour and at some time in spring of 1547, she secretly married him.

Katherine and Seymour's marriage has always been presented as a love match, that turned sour following his attentions to her step-daughter, but Porter contends that the match was not altogether without political motivation. Seymour was disgruntled at the speedy advance of his older brother, Edward Seymour, Earl of Hertford, who was now rapidly promoted to Duke of Somerset and Lord Protector by a coterie of his allies, who overthrew Henry's plans for a balanced Regency Council and arrogated the power (and a handsome round of titles and treasure) to themselves.

Sir Thomas Seymour received only the Baronetcy of Sudeley, and the continuation of his position as Lord High Admiral. Katherine, too, had her nose put out of joint by the loss of the position of Regent that she had probably expected. A marriage between the two of them, both of whom were loved by the young King, might enable them to regain influence.

The secret marriage shocked the court when it emerged – Katherine had married during a period when any pregnancy could (however unlikely) be the result of her marriage to Henry – this would throw a spanner into the succession. In particular, Lady Mary was hurt at the apparent disrespect to her father. However, Somerset and the rest of the Council had to accept a fait accompli, especially as Seymour had cleverly put the idea into young Edward VI's head that the marriage was his own idea. Edward, though, was as intelligent as all the rest of the Tudors and spotted that he had been manipulated, which did not endear the new couple to him further.

The early days of the marriage were overshadowed by an unseemly quarrel between Queen Katherine (as she was still addressed) and her new-sister-in-law, Anne Stanhope, Duchess of Somerset. Anne had been one of Katherine's inner, evangelical circle and one of her chief Ladies-in-waiting and there is no record of why they quarrelled, but now the fur really flew. The Duchess refused to carry the train of the former Queen, as she was now the wife of her husband's younger brother and wrote to her husband:

'If my Lord Admiral will teach his wife no better manners, I am she that will'.

Katherine was entitled to precedence as Queen on the strict instructions laid down in Henry's will, but was no match for the Duchess who jostled her in doorways. Katherine relieved her feelings by referring to the Duchess as *'that hell'*, (the word being the Tudor equivalent of c***) and saying she was so exasperated with the Duke that she could have *'bitten him'* when he refused to hand over her jewels.

Despite this family bickering, Katherine and Seymour were happily settled at Chelsea and Hanworth, Katherine's dower properties. The Lady Elizabeth formed part of her household, and Seymour purchased the wardship of Lady Jane Grey, on the promise to her father, Henry, Duke of Suffolk, that he would arrange a match between Lady Jane and her cousin, the King.

Sadly, Katherine's bubble was burst. Sir Thomas began to flirt, to use no stronger term, with Lady Elizabeth, visiting her in her bedchamber whilst she was still in bed, slapping and tickling her, to the horror of her governess, Mrs Ashley. Mrs Ashley remonstrated with him, but to no avail and eventually told the Queen. Katherine dealt with the matter by joining in, but the damage was done, and eventually, in the spring of 1548 Katherine felt compelled to send Lady Elizabeth away, to protect the girl's reputation. Katherine was now pregnant for the first time (so far as is known). She and Sir Thomas were thrilled beyond measure, and the level of affection in their letters suggests that the tricky incident with Lady Elizabeth was forgiven and forgotten.

Seymour spent vast sums on refurbishing his new castle of Sudeley for the birth of his heir (obviously a boy – all Tudor men thought their children would be male) and the couple moved there in June of 1548, accompanied by the young Jane Grey. Katherine spent the sunny days in her garden, with Jane by her side, further pleased by being reconciled with Lady Mary and on good terms with Lady Elizabeth again. There are no reports of any illness and when she went into labour in late August of 1548 there was no reason to expect anything but a happy outcome. Unfortunately, however, after the birth of a girl, named Mary, she contracted puerperal fever, and died on 5th September 1548. In her delirium she accused Seymour of mistreating her, but when she regained lucidity she bequeathed him all her possessions *wishing them a thousand times more*.

As was the custom, Seymour did not attend the funeral. The chief mourner was Lady Jane Grey, who followed the sad procession the 100 yards or so from the Queen's privy chamber to the Church. The service was the first Protestant burial of an English Queen – no prayers for the dead, the candles and offerings only for the honour of the late Queen, and with no other significance, the psalms and Te Deum in English.

She lies still under the stones of the church, with an alabaster monument placed over her in the nineteenth century.

Her little daughter, Mary, was orphaned in 1549 when Sir Thomas was executed. She was last heard of in the household of Katherine's friend, Katherine Willoughby, Duchess of Suffolk in 1550 and it seems probable that she died not long after.

Aspects of Katherine Parr's Life

Chapter 8: What did Katherine look like?

There are no detailed descriptions of Katherine in terms of height, hair, figure, eye colour and so on, but we are lucky that she was the most frequently painted of Henry's queens and there are various references to her in sources that, whilst they don't describe her in detail, give an impression of her looks and personality.

It seems reasonable to suppose that Katherine was attractive – Henry VIII was very susceptible to physical appearance, as his rejection of Anne of Cleves because he didn't fancy her, shows. However, she is not referred to as beautiful by any of the ambassadors sending reports, and, in fact, Anne of Cleves is reputed to have complained that Katherine was less good-looking that herself.

Perhaps her attraction lay in her vivacity and joie de vivre. She seems to have a been a lively woman, fond of dancing, music and general merrymaking with a taste for the sensual pleasures in life – fine clothes, magnificent jewellery and numerous pairs of shoes. Her favourite colours for clothes were crimson, black and violet. All royal colours, designed to impress onlookers as well as frame her own charms.

Her height has been variously described by her biographers as 5 foot 4 inches, or 5 foot 10 inches, based on the length of her coffin. The shorter height seems more likely, as 5 foot 10 inches would be exceptional for a woman at that time. Tall women, such as Marie de Guise and her daughter, Mary Queen of Scots, were remarked on. Katherine's hair, a lock of which is preserved at Sudeley Castle, appears to be of a dark blonde hue, and so far as can be told from the paintings, her eyes were hazel or brown.

The best-known, authenticated portrait is the one by Master William Scrots, now in the National Portrait Gallery. It was probably painted in 1546 and shows the Queen wearing a very fashionable bonnet, rather than the traditional, stiff hood headdress and a dress with one of the new upstanding medici collars that were coming into fashion in the late 1540s. It also shows Katherine in her favourite crimson. Another portrait, probably by Master John, which used to be named as Lady Jane Grey, has now been shown definitively to be of Katherine. It is full length, and shows the Queen in a square-cut, embroidered gown with long, furred sleeves and a beautiful crown brooch. A similar portrait, by Lucas Herenbout, now at Melton Constable, shows another equally ornate dress with a similar brooch.

Katherine was described in 1544 by de Gante, the Secretary to the Duke of Najera:

'She is of a lively and pleasing appearance and is praised as a virtuous woman. She was dressed in a robe of cloth of gold and a petticoat of brocade with sleeves lined with crimson satin and trimmed with three-piled crimson velvet. Her train was more than two yards long. Suspended from her neck were two crosses, and a jewel of very rich diamonds and in her head-dress were many and beautiful ones. Her girdle was of gold with large pendants.'

Chapter 9: Katherine Parr as Step-mother

Katherine Parr's role as a step-mother has always been seen as central to her life and her success as Queen. It seems clear from the records and extant correspondence that she had a warm relationship with all of her five step-children, with the possible exception of Lord Latimer's son,

John. Novels occasionally assert that she had step-children older than herself, but this is presumably based on the now discredited theory that her first husband was Sir Edward Burgh the elder, rather than his grandson of the same name.

Katherine's first experience of a maternal role would have been in 1534 when she travelled to Snape Castle as the wife of John Neville, 3rd Baron Latimer. Latimer had two children from his first marriage, John, later 4th Baron, and Margaret Neville. John was around 14 at the time of his father's third marriage and Margaret perhaps five years younger. They had already had a short experience of a step-mother, but Latimer's second wife died within two years of marriage, leaving no children of her own.

In an era when the vast majority of people were married at least twice, their father's remarriage cannot have surprised the Neville children. Katherine Parr, as a member of an important gentry family in the north, and a kinswoman, was an unexceptionable choice, and it appears that she took an immediate and active interest in the education of Margaret, winning a love and respect from the young girl that would last all of Margaret's short life.

It seems to have been rather different with John. His later history suggests that he was a violent man, and Katherine later wrote 'Younglings...are offended at small trifles, taking everything in evil part, grudging and murmuring against their neighbour...' which strongly suggests experience of a sulky teenager.

Nevertheless, whatever the difficulties of his adolescence, young John's wife, Lucy Somerset, was later appointed as one of Katherine's ladies-in-waiting.

The most terrifying incident in the lives of Katherine, Margaret and young John would have been the attack on Snape by the rebels in 1537. The three of them were alone and unprotected by Lord Latimer who had been commanded to London to explain himself to the King and Council and beg for pardon for his part in the Pilgrimage of Grace. Latimer wrote to his friend Norfolk, lamenting his inability to protect his family as he was ordered to Doncaster. In the event, he ignored his immediate orders and raced towards Snape to effect a rescue. By the time of his arrival, however, the rebels had left. Latimer departed again, to head for Pontefract, leaving Katherine and the children behind.

As was common at the time, Margaret had been betrothed young, to Ralph Bigod, a son of Sir Francis Bigod. Unfortunately, Sir Francis, although a reformer, was one of the ring leaders of a second wave of revolt after which it was unthinkable that Latimer, who was desperately trying to shore up relations with the King, would let the match go forward. We cannot know what Margaret's reactions were - she may have been sorry that her match to a man she knew had been broken off, perhaps to be replaced by a wedding to a complete stranger. Whatever her feelings, we can safely assume that Katherine was her support.

During the first years of queenship, Katherine was attended by Margaret Neville, but sadly the girl died in 1545, probably aged no more than twenty. In her will, she speaks her regard of Katherine, and the will itself, which strongly reflects the reformed religion, suggests that Katherine had influenced her religious views markedly.

Katherine's role as stepmother to Henry VIII's children was one of the most important of her life, and her relationship with Elizabeth, in particular, had a lasting effect on England.

There is no evidence as to whether Katherine and the Lady Mary were childhood friends, as is often stated in novels. Maud Parr had remained in Queen Katharine's household until 1531 and it is probably safe to assume that the two girls had at least met, but the extent of their acquaintanceship was likely to have been slight, especially give the four year age gap. Lady Mary had spent the years 1525-8 in Ludlow as *de facto*, if not *de jure*, Princess of Wales, and Katherine left the south in 1528 to be married. Nevertheless from early 1542 Lady Latimer appears to have been closely connected with the Lady Mary's household. Dr James states that Katherine was a member of the Princess' privy chamber, but Porter points out that there is no evidence of payment to Katherine in the princess' accounts.

Lady Mary was, of course, well acquainted with Katherine's siblings. Anne Parr had received gifts from her, and was mentioned as in attendance on her in 1543 and this may be how the women became reacquainted. Whenever it happened, it is clear that a warm friendship sprang up between the two women.

Mary was present at the marriage of her father to Katherine and appears to have spent a good deal of time with the new queen. In particular, they shared intellectual interests. Katherine promoted the translation of Erasmus' *Paraphrases of the Gospels* from Latin in to English, and persuaded Mary, as a very accomplished Latinist, to undertake the translation of St John. In a letter to Mary, regarding the work's publication, she encouraged the Princess to let the work go forward under her own name:

'You will, in my opinion, do a real injury, if you refuse to let it go down to posterity under the auspices of your own name, since you have undertaken so much labour in accurately translating it...'

These intellectual interests were also the basis of relationships with her other two new stepchildren. Prince Edward was not yet six when Katherine became his stepmother. Up until this point his elder sister had been the closest to a mother he had known, but even allowing for the epistolary style that seems ludicrously overblown to modern readers, it appears from the letters between Katherine and Edward that a genuine love sprang up. She wrote to him (when he was aged 8!)

'I affectionately and thoughtfully consider with what great love you attend both me, your mother, and scholarship, at the same time.'

He wrote to her in similar style.

'Most honourable and entirely beloved mother, I have me most humbly recommended to your grace with like thanks both that your grace did accept so gently my simple and rude letters, ...[and that you] give me so much comfort and encouragement to go forward..'

The level of influence Katherine had over the selection of tutors for the young Prince is uncertain. Certainly, all his tutors were men who reflected her religious views (which were decidedly more progressive than Henry's) but it is difficult to imagine that the King would have left the choice to her entirely. It may be, of course, that the tutors kept their more radical views under wraps during Henry's reign, and that we are looking at them with the benefit of hindsight.

Elizabeth too, was charmed by her new step-mother, and, it appears, strongly influenced by her (although it is interesting to note that later, when choosing a new tutor, she rejected Katherine's choice). Her letters are also deeply humble and flattering, and the effort she put in to translating her step-mother's writings into several languages, and embroidering a beautiful book cover for a presentation copy of her work, suggest genuine admiration.

But following Henry's death, Katherine's relationships with her royal step-children began to go awry. She and Seymour undoubtedly traded on young Edward's affection for them to manipulate him into supporting their marriage. Of course, no-one is perfect and it is understandable that Katherine would use every weapon she had to secure personal happiness following years of doing her duty, but it seems to have wounded Edward.

Mary, too, was hurt and offended by Katherine's hasty remarriage, feeling it showed a distinct lack of respect for her late father. So far as is known, the ladies did not meet again, although that they were reconciled is demonstrated by a letter written in summer of 1548 when Mary asks about Katherine's *'great belly'* and hopes to see her soon.

It is interesting to speculate on whether, had Katherine lived, she might have tempered Mary's zeal for reinstatement of the religious world of her childhood. It seems unlikely - many of Mary's friends and intimates were reformers but although they were never persecuted themselves, there is nothing to indicate they influenced her.

Katherine's relationship with Elizabeth, too, was irrevocably altered by her remarriage. Prior to Henry's death, Elizabeth spent time with her siblings at Hertford Castle or Hatfield; following it, she moved into the household of her step-mother. It is not clear why this was felt necessary: if the girl did not need supervision directly by her step-mother before Henry's death, then why after? One can only assume that it was the choice of both of them. For Elizabeth, the pleasure of a maternal relationship must have been great. And so, Elizabeth joined the Dowager Queen at Chelsea Manor, and then Hanworth, and all seemed set fair for a happy family life with her step-mother and new step-father, Sir Thomas Seymour, who secretly married the Dowager Queen in Spring of 1547.

However, into this paradise crept the serpent of temptation. Seymour, who should have known better, took to flirting, and, in its kindest light, indulging in excessively physical horse-play with the young princess. She was obviously thrilled, and, not the first adolescent girl to have a crush on an older man, responded, to the point where her governess, Katherine Ashley, felt obliged to remonstrate both with her and Seymour, and eventually, felt bound to inform the Queen.

Katherine must have been shattered. The match with Seymour had undoubtedly been based on sincere affection and the revelation that he was not only flirting behind her back, but that he was endangering the reputation of the King's sister – potentially a treasonable offence - must have hit her hard.

Initially, Katherine seems to have concluded that, by joining in the fun and games, it would take the heat and the sexual element out of the relationship between Seymour and Elizabeth, but it was too late. In due course, Katherine felt constrained to send Elizabeth to the house of Sir Anthony and Lady Denny, at Cheshunt, whilst she, herself, retired to Sudeley to await the birth of her child. Elizabeth, obviously shaken by events, quickly understood that her step-mother had done what was best, and wrote her a genuine letter of thanks.

During the last summer of her life, Katherine corresponded with both Mary and Elizabeth, and perhaps also with Edward, although no letters remain.

Despite the upheavals caused by her final marriage, the step-daughters who had loved and respected her, both wished her well and spoke of their affection for her.

There is no record of the responses of her step-children to Katherine's death. One can imagine Edward, only eleven, bravely bearing the demise of his dear '*mother*', and eliminating all public show of feeling, as he was later to do for the executions of his uncles.

For Mary, who had lost so many people she had loved, it was the passing of a dear friend, but for Elizabeth it was the loss of the only maternal affection she had ever known (although her governess, Katherine Ashley was very dear to her as well).

There is no evidence as to Elizabeth's immediate reactions, but surely her own success as Queen must owe something to the example set by Katherine and is Katherine Parr's greatest legacy.

Chapter 10: Katherine Parr's Spiritual Development and Religious Writings

Katherine Parr was the first Queen of England to publish a book. She was not the first royal woman to appear in print – her grandmother-in-law, Lady Margaret Beaufort, had translated and published '*The Mirror of Gold to the Sinful Soul*' in 1507. Queen Marguerite of Navarre, whose reforming influence on the young Anne Boleyn was so profound, had published a second translation of the same work into French, from its original Latin, in 1531.

Religious self-examination was all the rage amongst the educated women of the early sixteenth century, and Katherine was a worthy heir to the fashion. Nevertheless, it is apparent from her writings that her faith was a truly heart-felt matter. She seems to have undergone some sort of personal conversion experience which she wrote about - at great length and in language that to modern ears is excruciatingly self-abasing.

In her childhood, Katherine would have been brought up to practise the Catholic faith, as it had been understood for over fifteen hundred years in England. Emphasis was on obedience to the Church's teachings, the need for personal effort to achieve salvation and, at the heart of it all, the miracle of the Mass, where the bread and wine were actually (although not visibly) transmuted into the body and blood of Christ. However, with the growth of printing, and the increasing availability of ancient texts to scholars, many of the Church's teachings were being questioned. In particular, the great minds of the late fifteenth and early sixteenth century were exercised by the competing doctrines of Free Will and Justification by Faith Alone and their place in salvation. It is very likely that during Katherine's education, she would have heard discussion and debate on the topic – many people who continued to see themselves as good Catholics held opposing views.

Tangled up in the theological debate, were the more political issues of the power and corruption of the Church, which was also being questioned in the 1520s. No intelligent person could fail to be aware of the issues and, when Katherine was first married and went to live in Lincolnshire, she came under the influence of her father-in-law, Sir Thomas Burgh, who was a vocal supporter of Church reform. Whether she had any more than an intellectual interest in the issues at this point is unknown but it seems unlikely. She later wrote that *'[God] called me diversely, but, through frorwardness* [deliberate contrariness] *I would not answer.'*

Katherine's second marriage was to Lord Latimer, who was considered to be a religious conservative, and maintained a highly decorated chapel at Snape Castle, full of the images and relics that the reformers disliked. During this period, Katherine attended Mass several times a day. Nevertheless, the picture of the religious views surrounding her is not straightforward – Latimer betrothed his daughter to the son of Sir Francis Bigod, a well-known reformer. Katherine's uncle, Sir William Parr of Horton, her brother, William Parr, later Marquis of Northampton, and her sister, Anne, later Countess of Pembroke, all seem to have embraced reform – although the level of genuine religious conviction is hard to gauge.

By the early 1540s an unbridgeable gulf had opened up between the evangelicals of the early years who wanted reform of abuses within the Church, and the new Protestants, as they were increasingly called, who questioned the very foundation of Catholic faith. The Protestants could not accept that that the bread and wine actually changed into the body and blood of Christ during the Mass. This was not something that anyone was interested in compromising over, in a time when people believed there was one truth (their own). The increasing acrimony between the sides created two parties at Henry's court. What Katherine's exact position on this point of doctrine was in 1543 when she became

Queen is uncertain, but she was certainly known as a follower of the reforming group. A member of her Privy Chamber wrote:

> *'Her piety cherishes the religion....introduced, not without great labour, into the palace.'*

Henry VIII had always enjoyed theological discussion and research, even writing his own book, back in 1519 – *'Assertio Septem Sacrementorum Adversus Martinem Lutherum'.* It may be that a desire to develop an intellectual relationship with Henry and be good company was, as she implied later when he complained of her trying to lecture him, her initial reason for getting involved in theological study. It is realistic to suppose that she wanted to develop a bond with him that was not primarily physical. To begin with, Henry seems to have encouraged Katherine's interest in theology - until she began to contradict him too freely.

For by delving into these areas, her own emotional response to religion had been stimulated and was leading her to embrace the more personal relationship with God espoused by the Protestants.

One of the fundamental desires of the reformers, from the early evangelicals to the radical Protestants, had been for the Word of God to be available in English, and it is apparent from all of Katherine's activities, both as writer and patron, that this was a mission dear to her heart.

In April 1544, an English translation of Bishop Fisher of Rochester's Latin *'Prayers or Psalms taken out of Holy Scripture'* appeared. Despite appearing anonymously, this translation is attributed to Katherine by one of her biographers, Dr. Susan James, on three grounds in particular – the similarity of some of the wording to that used in Katherine's own later work; its regular publication with works she definitely wrote; and the bills for copies of books that might be this one. Another biographer, Dr Linda Porter, is a little more equivocal in attribution, but adduces a convincing reason for why it might have been done anonymously: Fisher had been executed by Henry VIII, causing shockwaves at home and abroad, so he was probably not a man to talk about too frequently or be seen emulating. Fisher was, of course, a martyr for the supremacy of the Catholic Church, and, if Katherine were his translator, that would tend to suggest a moderate theological position during the translation period.

From, perhaps, a personal translation, Katherine went on to be the moving spirit behind the publication of the English translation of Erasmus' *Paraphrases upon the New Testament*. The editor was Nicholas Udall – famous alike for his scholarship and his brutal sexual abuse of his pupils at Eton College. The translators were various – Katherine may have worked on the St Matthew personally, but her main contribution was in persuading well-known Latinists to take a share, including her step-daughter, the Lady Mary. The book went through numerous editions in the sixteenth century, from its initial publication in January 1548.

Katherine's first publication under her own name was on 6th November 1545 when a work entitled *'Prayers and Meditations'* appeared, a fairly anodyne collection of snippets from 'holy works'. It included the fifteenth century *'Imitation of Christ'* by Thomas a Kempis which had been a standard work of piety for the secular reader since the 1420s. The collection also included a prayer written for men to say before battle – directed at the army accompanying Henry VIII into France.

This work was then translated by Katherine's step-daughter, the Lady Elizabeth, aged thirteen, into Latin, French and Italian, and, encased in a beautifully embroidered cover of her own work, presented as a New Year gift to Elizabeth's father, Henry VIII.

Katherine's next and most ambitious personal project was the *'Lamentations of a Sinner'*. In the course of twelve prolix chapters with titles such as '*A Christian bewailing the miserable ignorance and blindness of men*', we follow a sincere retelling of her journey from being mired in '*foul, wicked, perverse and crooked ways*' via utter rejection of '*the Bishop of Rome [as] a persecutor of the gospel, and grace, a setter forth of all superstition and counterfeit holiness*' to the sunlit uplands of the doctrine of Justification by Faith '*...we be justified by the faith in Christ, and not by the deeds of the law.*'

These, and later passages that seem to go beyond Lutheranism and dabble with the even more radical Calvinism that was emanating from Geneva, were well beyond anything that Henry VIII would have countenanced, although he would have loved the paragraphs hailing him as a new Moses and praising his role in '*[delivering] us out of captivity and bondage...*'. The book was not published in Henry's lifetime, instead emerging in late 1547.

By that time, Katherine's enthusiasm for writing seems to have waned. Her biographers imply that her religious enthusiasm emanated from repressed sexuality that needed a channel for expression during her first three marriages, but that could blossom happily in her final marriage to Sir Thomas Seymour. However, even if such a Freudian analysis is correct, it cannot detract from the genuine faith of the Queen that appears in her work and her dedication to the cause of setting forth religion in the vernacular for all people to read.

Chapter 11: Following the Footsteps of Katherine Parr

Alone amongst Henry's wives, Katherine Parr had an experience of life that was not completely submerged in Court circles. Her upbringing and life before her marriage to Henry, at the age of about thirty-one, was spent in the manors and castles of the gentry families of the Midlands and North of England. Whilst one could never say she knew what "ordinary" life was like, she was very much closer to it than any of Henry's other Queens, having been mistress of a country household, as well as of a great castle. She would have practised the housewifely skills of domestic economy, management of servants, preparation and administration of medicine and supervision of an estate that were the province of the wives and daughters of the gentry class. Thus, when we look at the places in which she lived, we can feel a faint breathe of daily life, which is denied us when we only look at palaces.

It is likely that Katherine was born at her parents' home in Blackfriars, although there is a slight possibility that the event took place at Fenel's Grove, near Great Kimble in Aylesbury, which her parents had possession of during the year of her birth. Blackfriars certainly seems to have been the place her parents considered as home, as they both chose to be buried in the Church of the Dominicans there. When the monasteries were dissolved the church, too, disappeared, to be replaced by St Ann's Blackfriars which, in turn, burnt down during the Great Fire. The Churchyard of St Ann's Blackfriars is now a garden, and is as close as we can get to the Parrs' tomb.

It is possible, although not likely, that Katherine visited the Court whilst her mother was in attendance on the Queen. In the early years of Henry's reign, he and Katharine of Aragon spent the majority of their time at Greenwich, Westminster, and the new palace built at Beaulieu. Hampton Court, of course, was not yet a royal residence.

After the death of Katherine's father, Sir Thomas Parr, in 1517 the young Parrs moved to live at Rye House, near Hoddesdon in Hertfordshire, in the household of their uncle, Sir William Parr of Horton, and his wife, Mary Salisbury. The Gatehouse, giving a clue to the red brick construction, remains and can be visited on a few days each year. The Parrs of Horton had four daughters of a similar age to the Parr siblings, and there were a number of other cousins and young men in the household, under the supervision of Katherine's mother, Maud, Lady Parr.

At the age of about sixteen, Katherine set out on a long journey to the northern part of Lincolnshire, to marry Edward Burgh. The journey, of some 135 miles would probably have taken around 10 days to two weeks, depending on the route taken, and the time of year. The obvious route, which we can follow today is up the Great North Road (the A1). A detour may have been made into Northamptonshire to visit other family members. There was a whole cluster of cousins, the Vaux, the Cheyneys and the Throckmortons, settled in that county, not far from the road north.

On reaching Newark, the party would have had the choice of turning off the Great North Road to visit Lincoln, which, with its Cathedral and Castle was a major town. Given that the itinerary followed by Henry VIII on his Northern Progress in the 1540s stopped at Lincoln, before proceeding to Gainsborough, we may infer that that is the route used at the time. Otherwise, Katherine's party would have continued north, turning off the Great North Road, as the modern traveller does, onto what is now the A1133 to Gainsborough.

When Katherine arrived in Gainsborough she is likely to have felt quite at home in the delightful modern manor house, Gainsborough Hall, that had been built by her new husband's great-grandfather, some sixty years earlier. For the modern visitor, the area is quite built up, but in the 1520s the whole area was still heavily forested.

Katherine lived for some time with her in-laws, but then her husband, Edward, was granted the Stewardship of the Manor of the Soke of Kirton-in-Lindsey. It was granted in survivorship (ie both parties retained the position until the death of the second) with his father Sir Thomas Burgh. Katherine and Edward would have travelled the twenty or so miles to the north-east of Gainsborough to take up residence. Today, there is a direct road between Gainsborough and Kirton, but even now it winds and twists, and five hundred years ago it was probably a difficult journey. Katherine may have been relieved that her in-laws could not visit too easily.

Kirton, set on an escarpment, overlooks the Lincolnshire Wolds. There is no trace of the house she would have lived in, the only current building of the time being the Church of St Andrew, where, no doubt, she and Edward would have worshipped.

On her widowhood in 1533, after four years in Lincolnshire, it is likely that Katherine journeyed across the Pennines to Sizergh Castle, Kendal to stay with her relative, Katherine Neville, Lady Strickland.

This would have been an arduous journey – further up the Great North Road, then either west to the south of the Pennines on what is now the A65, or north to Richmond, and then across on the route that is now the A66, or possibly even over the fells on what is now the A684. If she took this latter route (which is highly recommended as the views are fabulous) then she might have broken her journey at Snape Castle, home of her distant cousin, Sir John Neville, 3rd Baron Latimer.

Katherine's time at Sizergh would have been her first sojourn in a castle – dating from the 1300s it is significantly older than her previous homes. Her life there is likely to have encompassed visits to Kendal, the ancestral home of her father, although falling into disrepair by the 1530s. She may well have worshipped in the Church of the Holy Trinity in Kendal, where her grandfather's tomb can still be seen.

Whether Katherine was already acquainted with Lord Latimer is unknown, however at some point in 1533 she agreed to marry him and travelled the 50 miles back across the Pennines to Snape Castle.

Leaving Kendal for Snape nowadays, your Sat Nav will try to take you via the motorway, but overrule it and take the A684 (assuming that the weather is not icey in which case the road should be avoided as it is narrow and steep.) The route is a marvellous trek up and down the Lakeland fells and into the North York moors. If Lord Latimer came courting the widowed Mistress Burgh in 1533, this is the route he would have taken, and this is the route his bride would have ridden as she said goodbye to Lady Strickland and headed east to her new home.

Around 10 miles West of the Great North road, now the A1, but following the old Roman route and the main artery between York and London, Katherine would have turned off towards Snape, and just as it does today, the road passed Jervaulx Abbey, the lordship of which had passed to her father when he inherited his mother's moiety of the Barony of FitzHugh of Ravensworth. Whether Katherine would have wanted to visit the Abbey may depend on how advanced her religious views had become. In 1533, although some of the smaller houses had been closed by Cardinal Wolsey because of lack of numbers, there was no breath of the massive programme of dissolution that would overwhelm the country, changing it more in the following five years than in the previous five hundred.

Arriving at Snape, she would have found a new home very much grander than her old manor at Kirton-in-Lindsey, or even Gainsborough Hall. The fifteenth century castle had been built as one of the great Neville strongholds and commanded a large area of countryside.

Nowadays, Snape, and its attendant villages of Snape and Wells, seem very isolated, but in Katherine's day the route between Ripon and Jervaulx was well travelled, and there were many castles and manors in the surrounding area lived in by her various cousins – the Scrope castle of Bolton (which might have been her home had her mother's original marriage plans for her to the Scrope heir been fulfilled), and the royal castles of Sheriff Hutton and Middleham are all within a day's ride.

The church associated with the Latimers - St Michael and All Angels, Well - is less than three miles away, and would have been patronised by Katherine and her new Neville family.

However, her country life was rudely interrupted by the Pilgrimage of Grace. Following the suppression of the rebellion, and the reluctant pardoning of her husband for his part in it, according to her biographer, Katherine and Latimer moved south, first to Wick Manor in Worcestershire, and then to the bosom of her family in Northamptonshire.

From Snape to Wick is not an easy journey, even now. The easiest route is to rejoin the A1 at Kirklingon and then follow it south to Doncaster where you turn west onto the M18 to link up with the M1 southbound. The M1 will take you to the A42, and thence to the M42 and M5 south to Worcestershire. Exiting the M5 onto the A449, follow the road through the lovely market town of Pershore (famous for its plums!).

Pershore and its environs grew up around the great Abbey Church of the Holy Cross, which, when the Latimers arrived had not yet been dissolved.

Wick is on the eastern edge of Pershore, down a signposted side road. In fact, the manor of Wick belonged to Latimer's brother, William, in right of his wife, so the trip may have been more in the nature of a family visit, and perhaps a welcome oasis of tranquillity, as Worcestershire had played no part in the Pilgrimage of Grace.

There are many traces of mediaeval and Tudor buildings incorporated into current houses in the village, but the masterpiece is the one known as Wick Manor, which at first glance is the quintessence of a Tudor Manor House, but in fact it was almost completely rebuilt in the early twentieth century.

The Latimers did not remain long in Wick. According to his biographers, Lord Latimer then purchased a property called Stowe Manor in Northamptonshire, in the village of Church Stowe (also known as Stowe IX Churches). However, this property had previously belonged to his great-grandmother, Eleanor Beauchamp, and passed to his great-aunt, Katherine Neville, Lady Dudley. It seems likely that the reversion of the estate had fallen to Lord Latimer, rather than him needing to buy it. The remains of the Tudor Manor are incorporated in a more modern building. Katherine was granted a life interest in Stowe Manor on Latimer's death. Church Stowe is located on the A5, about 10 miles west of Northampton.

In addition, on consulting maps, and the History of Northamptonshire, it appears that Latimer had another manor at Burton Latimer, just south of Kettering, which is within 5 miles of the manors of Orlingbury and Harrowden, inhabited by Katherine's cousins, Maud Parr, Lady Lane, and Elizabeth Cheyney, Lady Vaux, where they may have spent time, although there is no trace of a house there of the right size or age.

The Church at Burton Latimer, however, remains as does that of Harrowden. The Orlingbury Hall Katherine would have known was demolished and rebuilt in 1709 and Orlingbury Church was also rebuilt in the nineteenth century. The Vaux Manor of Harrowden was completely rebuilt in the 18th Century. It now houses the Wellingborough Golf Club. From Burton Latimer, take the A509 towards Wellingborough, from which Harrowden and Orlingbury are signposted, Harrowden is actually on the main road, and Orlingbury a mile off it.

Katherine's uncle, Sir William Parr of Horton, lived about 15 miles from this cluster of family. No traces of his home remain, although he and his wife are commemorated in the Church of St Mary Magdalene – not open other than on Sundays. Horton may be reached from

Orlingbury by rejoining the A509 South, then turning onto the A428, then following the signposts onto the B526 Newport Pagnell Road.

Katherine would not, however, have remained at home all of the time. Latimer was called to various commissions for the suppression of the recent rebels, and she is likely to have accompanied him to York.

Finally, the Latimers moved to their house in Charterhouse Yard, London, presumably a house near the great Carthusian Monastery that had been one of the most resistant to the Dissolution. Latimer died here, and Katherine moved to Court, visiting or employed by the Lady Mary.

When Katherine married Henry in 1543 she would have found herself in previously unparalleled luxury and opulence, Hampton Court, Greenwich Palace, Oatlands and Nonsuch would all have been visited regularly. In addition, there were the smaller palaces and castles, such as Hertford Castle, where she visited the young Prince of Wales or the various hunting lodges that Henry favoured.

There was the Tower of London, still officially a Palace, although not much used as such by the end of Henry's reign and the mediaeval Westminster Palace, of which the 14th century hall (Westminster Hall) is the only remaining part.

Henry's new palace of Whitehall, the redbrick St James Palace and the mighty Windsor Castle were also Katherine's homes during her time as Queen.

On Henry's death, Katherine received the Manors of Chelsea and Hanworth. Neither of these exists any longer. Chelsea Place (as it was properly known) was built in the early 1500s, facing the riverside, under the current 19-26 Cheyne Walk. It was updated in the 1600s, then demolished in the late 1750s.

In the summer of 1548, Katherine travelled to what was to be her last home, Sudeley Castle in Gloucestershire, which had been granted to her fourth husband, the new King's uncle, Thomas Seymour. Seymour spent significant sums on renovating it and laying out gardens for the Queen's pleasure and we may imagine her, enjoying her beautiful surroundings as she awaited the birth of her first child. Unfortunately, Katherine died in childbirth and was laid to rest in the church at Sudeley.

Key to Map

1. Jervaulx Abbey
2. Hertford
3. Kendal
4. Sizergh Castle
5. Snape Castle
6. Sudeley Castle
7. Tower of London
8. Windsor Castle
9. St Paul's Cathedral
10. Holy Trinity, Kendal
11. St Andrews, Kirton-in-Lindsey
12. St Ann, Blackfriars
13. St Mary Magdalene, Horton
14. Chelsea Manor
15. Gainsborough Old Hall
16. Greens Norton Manor
17. Hanworth Manor
18. Harrowden Hall
19. Kirton-in-Lindsey
20. Rye House
21. Stansted Hall
22. Greenwich
23. Hampton Court
24. Nonsuch Palace
25. Oatlands Palace

26. Richmond Palace
27. Westminster Palace
28. Whitehall Palace

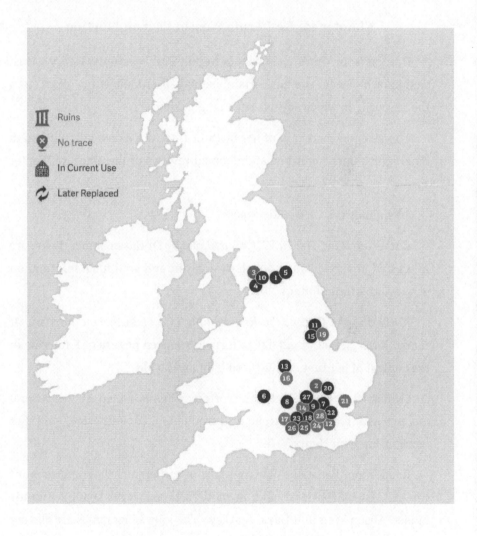

Chapter 12: Katherine Parr in Fact and Fiction

If, as is sometimes claimed, Katherine Parr was once Henry's least well known Queen, she has certainly emerged in the last few years from the obscurity in which she has been languishing.

To mark the centenary of her birth in 1512, three detailed, full-length biographies were published and detailed reviews of these are in Chapter 13.

To summarise, we would suggest:

Catherine Parr, Henry VIII's Last Love by Dr Susan James, if you are interested in very detailed, scholarly analysis and additional information about Katherine's siblings.

Katherine the Queen, the Remarkable Life of Katherine Parr by Dr Linda Porter, if you would like to form a balanced picture of Katherine in the context of her time, seeing both light and shade.

Catherine Parr by Elizabeth Norton. This is aimed at the general reader, and forms an excellent introduction to Katherine, and her relationship with Henry VIII.

In addition, Katherine plays her part in earlier joint biographies by, of course, Agnes Strickland, and, in modern times David Loades, Antonia Fraser, Alison Weir and David Starkey. The joint biographies are all very different in tone.

Lives of the Queens of England, Vol V by Agnes Strickland. This classic work in thirteen volumes was first published in the 1840s and has been referred to by every biographer of queens thereafter. Miss

Strickland, who moved in very exalted circles, had access to huge quantities of original papers and letters. She is a sympathetic portraitist of all of the queens, and is particularly attached to Katherine Parr, because of the relationship of the Parrs to her own Strickland ancestors. Although superseded in many ways, it is still worth reading for atmosphere and the human touch.

The Six Wives of Henry VIII by Alison Weir. Weir's book was published back in 1991, before the extensive research undertaken by Dr James was available. It is therefore reliant upon earlier research, particularly Strickland's rather romantic stories and perpetuates the myth of the nurse. Interestingly, however, Weir correctly identifies the portrait once labelled Lady Jane Grey, but now proved conclusively by James to be of Katherine Parr. Weir has not received (so far as we aware) any credit for this early identification.

The Six Wives of Henry VIII by Dr David Starkey. Dr Starkey's work is as challenging to received opinion as most of his books. As a worshipper of Henry VIII, he sees Henry's wives only as adjuncts to the great man, rather than having much of an interest in the ladies themselves. He does, however, raise a very interesting point around the possibility that Katherine's religious views were influenced by Sir Francis Bigod, which has been taken up vigorously by Elizabeth Norton.

The Six Wives of Henry VIII by Antonia Fraser. Although published more than twenty years ago, this has stood the test of time well. Fraser manages to convey a wealth of information in a very readable format. All of the key information about Katherine is here, and some interesting comparisons with Henry's other wives.

The Tudor Queens of England by Dr David Loades. Dr Loades' slim volume covers thirteen queens in a mere 220 or so pages, so cannot be expected to be a detailed account. In fact, the only details Dr Loades seems much interested in relate to Katherine's sex life. In the four pages devoted to her, he manages to mention that she was sexually frustrated on each one (although how he knows this is a mystery.) He is dismissive of her role as Regent, and scathing about her writings.

The Six Wives and Many Mistresses of Henry VIII by *Amy Licence*. This work concentrates solely on the personal relationships between the King and his various love interests. By the time he was married to Katherine Parr, the fires of passion were somewhat dimmed, although there is no question that he consummated the marriage. There were rumours that she would be replaced by her friend, Katherine Willoughby, Duchess of Suffolk, but Katherine Parr continued to please him enough to keep her place.

Katherine appears fairly frequently in fictional accounts. She is the main protagonist in:

The Queen's Gambit by Elizabeth Freemantle. This is well written fiction with the facts and interpretation largely drawn from the James biography.

The Taming of the Queen by Philippa Gregory. This is the latest in the best-selling author's series on the Tudor Court

The Sixth Wife by Suzanne Dunn. The very modern idiom takes a bit of getting used to, but it is well done. The novel centres, in fact on Katherine's friend, the Duchess of Suffolk, but, without giving too much away, Katherine Parr is an equally important character.

The Sixth Wife by Jean Plaidy – a bit out of date now, but always readable. It is also available in Audio.

Katherine also makes an appearance in the following books.

Heartstone and its sequel *Lamentation* by C J Sansom. Sansom has done a truly exceptional job of bringing the later years of Henry VIII alive. Katherine is an important and sympathetic character.

The Dark Rose by Cynthia Harrod-Eagles

The classic *Young Bess* by Margaret Irwin

The sadly out of print *I am Mary Tudor* by Hilda Lewis

Chapter 13: Katherine Parr: Three Book Reviews

Katherine the Queen: The Remarkable Life of Katherine Parr

Author: Dr Linda Porter

Publisher: MacMillan 19 March 2010

In a nutshell: A beautifully written account, with interesting new interpretations for the expert as well as a wealth of information for the generalist.

This is a very well balanced and informative book. Porter clearly admires Katherine, her intellect, her passion for learning, her ability to adapt to circumstances, but she does not allow Katherine's strong points to completely overshadow the less attractive elements of her character – her reluctance to pay her bills and her rather cynical manipulation of her step-son, Edward VI's, affections in her and Seymour's bid to have their marriage recognised, are noted. She also reads Katherine's very unkind letter to Lady Wriothesley, on the death of the lady's child, at face value and does not try to soften it.

Porter's underlying theme seems to be that Katherine, like all good daughters of a Tudor family was aiming for familial power: if possible, through a child of her own, and if not, through her influence over her step-children and the promotion of her relatives and servants.

Porter gives a new interpretation of Katherine's relationship with her fourth husband, Thomas Seymour. Acknowledging it to be a love match, she also speculates on it as a considered and deliberate route for both to achieve their joint ambitions of control of the minority government of Edward VI. Katherine, disappointed of the Regency by Henry VIII's final Will, wanted to retain influence in the new regime, and a marriage to the new King's uncle would improve her ability to stay close to the King. Unfortunately, she appears to have reckoned without Seymour's poor judgement and the sibling rivalry between the Seymour brothers.

As well as the wider issue of power politics and factionalism in the Tudor court, Porter concentrates on Katherine's journey from traditional faith to evangelism, and her strong influence over her step daughter, Elizabeth.

Porter never goes beyond the facts. In the debate about whether Katherine served in the household of Mary Tudor in the period around and after the death of Lord Latimer, she clearly identifies that there is no record of Katherine in Mary's accounts as an official member of the Princess' household. The evidence of an order for dresses and jewellery for the Princess issued by Katherine to be paid for by the King's accounts department she accounts for as an activity that any of Mary's friends or subordinates might have carried out for her, especially as Mary and Katherine were both lovers of fine clothes and jewels. However, this faithfulness to what can be proven does not make for a dull book, because Porter uses her facts to draw interesting inferences and interpretations that are new.

For example, the reconsideration of Katherine's physical relationship with Henry: the old Victorian idea that Katherine was merely his nurse has long been dismissed, but Porter argues for a determined effort by Katherine to keep the King sexually satisfied, citing the frequent purchases of perfumes, body lotions, flowers for her bedchamber and beautiful and sensual clothes as her efforts to keep him motivated.

*

Catherine Parr: Henry VIII's Last Love

Author: Dr Susan James

Publisher: The History Press

In a nutshell: For a reader who is interested in details and academic analysis, but also wants to gain an insight into Katherine's own tastes and habits.

Dr James has undertaken a vast amount of research and probably wins the title of 'scholarly biography' for this work.

There is no factual detail about Queen Katherine that she has not investigated. She has looked into her clothes, her jewels, her books, her clocks and her pets, and we emerge with a very definite feeling for Katherine's tastes and pastimes. James has effectively established the true identity of Katherine's first husband and dispelled the myths of him being an old man, although she perhaps draws stronger conclusions from the evidence on some matters than Porter does.

James clearly admires Katherine hugely and seems to identify with her emotionally – balancing on the point where any further empathy would tip her over into emotional invention. For example, with reference to a letter to Lady Wriothesley, purporting to be one of condolence on the loss of her child, when Katherine's injunctions to the lady to accept God's Will seem hard-hearted, even allowing for the religious views of the age, James defends Katherine's unkindness by referring to the lady's grief as hysterical.

James has also done extremely detailed work in investigating Katherine's religious writings, undertaking minute analysis of the structure and style of the works to establish likely authorship of previously uncertain attributions.

Also interesting and informative is the picture that emerges of Katherine's siblings, in particular William Parr, Marquis of Northampton. Again, meticulous research has paid dividends.

There are one or two bizarre mistakes of fact in relation to people other than Katherine herself. James refers on two occasions to Sir Edward Baynton, Anne Boleyn's Chamberlain, as Anne's brother-in-law – apparently married to her half-sister. If Anne Boleyn had a half-sister, only Dr James has ever heard of her. Anne Boleyn's brothers-in-law were the two husbands of her sister Mary, William Carey and William Stafford. James also quotes a description of Matthew, Earl of Lennox, as a 'lusty, lady-faced boy', a description that was, in fact, made of Lennox's son, Lord Darnley, some twenty years later.

But these oddities and a few editing quibbles (the constant confusion of the word tenet with tenant, giving us tenants of religion, was particularly irritating) do not detract from a really thorough and detailed account of Katherine Parr's life from cradle to grave.

*

Catherine Parr: Wife, Widow, Mother, Survivor. The Story of the Last Wife of Henry VIII

Author: Elizabeth Norton

Publisher: Amberley Publishing 4 January 2010

In a nutshell: A good introduction to the topic, covering the main aspects of Katherine Parr's life, with plenty of interpretation.

Norton has produced a series of works on the wives of Henry VIII, in which she concentrates on the Queens' own perspectives on life, with plenty of biographical detail, rather than the wider historical context.

Her work on Katherine Parr covers all of the events of her life, and attempts to draw conclusions about the Queen's own emotional or practical response to the turmoil that surrounded the Tudor gentry and nobility.

Whilst Norton has clearly benefited from Dr James' research, she draws her own conclusions from the information – for example, her views on Katherine's level of education and skill in languages differ from those of James, but are certainly very credible, and perhaps more likely.

More than any other of Katherine's biographers, Norton concludes quite definitely that Katherine's evangelical religion dated from her first marriage to Edward Burgh, when she came under the influence of Edward's father, a noted reformer. Whereas Dr Starkey infers that exposure to Lord Latimer's reformist friend, Sir Francis Bigod, may have influenced Katherine, Norton implies that it was Katherine who encouraged the friendship between the men, and the proposed match between Bigod's son and Latimer's daughter.

Norton explores the relationships Katherine had with Latimer's wider family – identifying the risks the couple were exposed to by the potentially treasonous activities of Latimer's brothers, William and Marmaduke. She notes, however, that Katherine must have had a soft spot for Marmaduke (*Ed - if only for his name!*) appointing him to a place in her household, once Queen.

Norton quite rightly identifies when an event is possible, but not proven. However, she sometimes then goes on to draw very definite conclusions from that event. An example is her use of the *Legend of Sir Nicholas Throckmorton* to demonstrate Katherine's reputation for helping her friends and family. She gives convincing reasons why the *Legend* may be accurate, whilst pointing out that it was written after Katherine had become Queen, so composed with the benefit of hindsight. In one paragraph she writes 'It is therefore not impossible that Catherine (sic) could have secured an audience with the king...' then on the next page says 'This is the first recorded meeting between Catherine and Henry.'

Katherine's reformist religious views are explored at length, and Norton gives her a very proactive role in shaping the religious position of her step-daughter, later Elizabeth I.

This is a very readable work (although it might benefit from more rigorous editing) and would be a welcome addition to a reader seeking a wide range of interpretations of Katherine's life.

Bibliography

The works listed below were consulted for several of the Profiles with more specific works related to the individuals listed under their names.

Calendar of State Papers: Domestic Series: Edward VI, 1547-1553. United Kingdom: Stationery Office Books.

Calendar of State Papers Simancas, British History Online (HMSO, 1892) Hume, Martin A S, ed.,

Calendar of State Papers: Venice <http://www.british-history.ac.uk/cal-state-papers/venice/vol2/vii-lxi> [accessed 7 October 2015]

Cecil Papers, http://www.british-history.ac.uk/cal-cecil-papers (Accessed: 7 September 2015)

Letters and Papers, Foreign and Domestic, of the Reign of Henry VIII: Preserved in the Public Record Office, the British Museum, and Elsewhere in England (United Kingdom: British History Online, 2014) https://www.british-history.ac.uk/letters-papers-hen8/ Brewer, John Sherren, and James Gairdner,

De Lisle, Leanda, *Tudor: The Family Story* (United Kingdom: Chatto & Windus, 2013)

Ellis, Henry, *Original Letters, Illustrative of English History: Including Numerous Royal Letters: From Autographs in the British Museum, the State Paper Office, and One or Two Other Collections.*, 1st edn (New York: Printed for Harding, Triphook, & Lepard, 1824)

Foxe, John, *The Acts and Monuments of John Foxe: A New and Complete Edition: With a Preliminary Dissertation by the Rev. George Townsend* (London: R.R. Seeley and W. Burnside, 1837)

Fraser, Antonia, *The Six Wives of Henry VIII*, First (London: Weidenfeld & Nicolson, 1992)

Hall, Edward, *Hall's Chronicle.* (S.l.: Ams Press, 1909)

Hayward, Maria, ed., *The Great Wardrobe Accounts of Henry VII and Henry VIII* (United Kingdom: London Record Society, 2012)

Holinshed, Raphael, *Holinshed's Chronicles of England, Scotland & Ireland* (United Kingdom: AMS Press, 1997)

Ives, Eric, *Lady Jane Grey: A Tudor Mystery*, 1st edn (United Kingdom: Wiley-Blackwell (an imprint of John Wiley & Sons Ltd), 2012)

James, Susan E., *Catherine Parr: Henry VIII's Last Love* (United Kingdom: Tempus Publishing, 2008)

Jerdan, William, ed., *Rutland Papers. Original Documents Illustrative of the Courts and Times of Henry VII. and Henry VIII. Selected from the Private Archives of His Grace the Duke of Rutland* (Leopold Classic Library, 2015)

Lemon, Robert, ed., *Calendar of State Papers: Domestic Series: Edward, Mary and Elizabeth,* British History Online (London: HMSO, 1856)

Morse H., *Select Documents Of English Constitutional History*, ed. by George Burton Adams and Morse H Stephens (United States: Kessinger Publishing, 2007)

Norton, Elizabeth, *Catherine Parr* (United Kingdom: Casemate Pub & Book Dist, 2010)

Porter, Linda, *Katherine the Queen: The Remarkable Life of Katherine Parr,* Kindle (Macmillan, 2010)

Starkey, David, *Six Wives of Henry VIII* (London: Vintage, 2004)

Strype, John, Annals of the Reformation and Establishment of Religion and Other Various Occurrences in the Church of England Etc. (Oxford: Clarendon Press, 1824),

Vergil, Polydore, *Anglica Historia AD 1485-1637* (Royal Historical, 1950)

Weir, Alison, *Henry VIII: King and Court* (London: Jonathan Cape, 2001)

Weir, Alison, *The Six Wives of Henry VIII*, 1st edn (London: Random House UK Distribution, 1991)

Williams, Neville, *Henry VIII and His Court.* (London: Littlehampton Book Services, 1971)

Printed in Great Britain
by Amazon